WITHDRAWN
UTSA LIBRARIES

Also by Frederick Seidel

FINAL SOLUTIONS
SUNRISE
POEMS, 1959–1979

THESE DAYS

THESE DAYS

Frederick Seidel

NEW POEMS

ALFRED A. KNOPF   NEW YORK

1989

THIS IS A BORZOI BOOK
PUBLISHED BY ALFRED A. KNOPF, INC.

Copyright © 1980, 1981, 1982, 1983, 1984, 1986, 1987, 1988, 1989 by Frederick Seidel

All rights reserved under International and Pan-American Copyright Conventions. Published in the United States by Alfred A. Knopf, Inc., New York, and simultaneously in Canada by Random House of Canada Limited, Toronto. Distributed by Random House, Inc., New York.

The poems in this book were originally published in *Almanacco dello Specchio* (Arnoldo Mondadori Editore, Milan), *The New York Review of Books*, *Nuovi Argomenti* (Rome), *The Paris Review*, and *Raritan*. *The American Poetry Review:* "On Wings of Song" and "The Last Poem in the Book." *Antaeus:* "The New Cosmology." *London Review of Books:* "Scotland" (Vol. 2, No. 11), "The Blue-Eyed Doe" (Vol. 6, No. 1), and "Gethsemane" (Vol. 9, No. 2). Some of the same poems were subsequently published in *Men and Woman: New and Selected Poems* (Chatto & Windus, London, 1984).

Frontispiece: *Alle de werken van den Heere Jacob Cats*, after Adriaen van de Venne, Amsterdam, 1712, "Sufficit una." Print Collection, Miriam & Ira D. Wallach Division of Art, Prints and Photographs. The New York Public Library, Astor, Lenox and Tilden Foundations.

Library of Congress Cataloging-in-Publication Data
Seidel, Frederick, [date]
    These days : poems / by Frederick Seidel. — 1st ed.
       p.   cm.
    ISBN 0-394-58022-2 — ISBN 0-679-72651-9 (pbk.)
    I. Title.
PS3569.E5T48   1989
811'.54—dc20   89-45296   CIP

Manufactured in the United States of America
First Edition

Library
University of Texas
at San Antonio

CONTENTS

THESE DAYS

SCOTLAND

A stag lifts his nostrils to the morning
In the crosshairs of the scope of love,
And smells what the gun calls Scotland and falls.
The meat of geology raw is Scotland: Stone
Age hours of stalking, passionate aim for the heart,
Bleak dazzling weather of the bare and green.
Old men in kilts, their beards are lobster-red.
Red pubic hair of virgins white as cows.
Omega under Alpha, rock hymen, fog penis—
The unshaved glow of her underarms is the sky
Of prehistory or after the sun expands.

The sun will expand a billion years from now
And burn away the mist of Caithness—till then,
There in the Thurso phone book is Robin Thurso.
But he is leaving for his other castle.
"Yes, I'm just leaving—what a pity! I can't
Remember, do you shoot?" Dukes hunt stags,
While Scotsmen hunt for jobs and emigrate,
Or else start seeing red spots on a moor
That flows to the horizon like a migraine.
Sheep dot the moor, bubblebaths of unshorn
Curls somehow red, unshepherded, unshorn.

Gone are the student mobs chanting the *Little Red
Book* of Mao at their Marxist dons.
The universities in the south woke,
Now they are going back to the land of dreams—
Tour buses clog the roads that take them there.
Gone, the rebel psychoanalysts.
Scotland trained more than its share of brilliant ones.
Pocked faces, lean as wolves, they really ran
To untrain and be famous in London, doing wild
Analysis, vegetarians brewing
Herbal tea for anorexic girls.

Let them eat haggis. The heart, lungs and liver
Of a sheep minced with cereal and suet,
Seasoned with onions, and boiled in the sheep's stomach.
That's what the gillie eats, not venison,
Or salmon, or grouse served rare, not for the gillie
That privilege, or the other one which is
Mushed vegetables molded to resemble a steak.
Let them come to Scotland and eat blood
Pud from a food stall out in the open air,
In the square in Portree. Though there is nothing
Better in the world than a grouse cooked right.

They make a malt in Wick that tastes as smooth
As Mouton when you drink enough of it.
McEwen adored both, suffered a partial stroke,
Switched to champagne and died. A single piper
Drones a file of mourners through a moor,
The sweet prodigal being piped to his early grave.
A friend of his arriving by helicopter
Spies the procession from a mile away,
The black speck of the coffin trailing a thread,
Lost in the savage green, an ocean of thawed
Endlessness and a spermatozoon.

A vehement bullet comes from the gun of love.
On the island of Raasay across from Skye,
The dead walk with the living hand in hand
Over to Hallaig in the evening light.
Girls and boys of every generation,
MacLeans and MacLeods, as they were before they were
Mothers and clansmen, still in their innocence,
Walk beside the islanders, their descendants.
They hold their small hands up to be held by the living.
Their love is too much, the freezing shock-alive
Of rubbing alcohol that leads to sleep.

FLAME

The honey, the humming of a million bees,
In the middle of Florence pining for Paris;
The whining trembling the cars and trucks hum
Crossing the metal matting of Brooklyn Bridge
When you stand below it on the Brooklyn side—
High above you, the harp, the cathedral, the hive—
In the middle of Florence. Florence in flames.

Like waking from a fever . . . it is evening.
Fireflies breathe in the gardens on Bellosguardo.
And then the moon steps from the cypresses and
A wave of feeling breaks, phosphorescent—
Moonlight, a wave hushing on a beach.
In the dark, a flame goes out. And then
The afterimage of a flame goes out.

OUR GODS

Older than us, but not by that much, men
Just old enough to be uncircumcised,
Episcopalians from the Golden Age
Of schools who loved to lose gracefully and lead—
Always there before us like a mirage,
Until we tried to get closer, when they vanished,
Always there until they disappeared.

They were the last of a race, that was their cover—
The baggy tweeds. Exposed in the Racquet Club
Dressing room, they were invisible,
Present purely in outline like the head
And torso targets at the police firing
Range, hairless bodies and full heads of hair,
Painted neatly combed, of the last WASPs.

They walked like boys, talked like their grandfathers—
Public servants in secret, and the last
Generation of men to prefer baths.
These were the CIA boys with EYES
ONLY clearance and profiles like arrowheads.
A fireside frost bloomed on the silver martini
Shaker the magic evenings they could be home.

They were never home, even when they were there.
Public servants in secret are not servants,
Either. They were our gods working all night
To make Achilles' beard fall out and prop up
The House of Priam, who by just pointing sent
A shark fin gliding down a corridor,
Almost transparent, like a watermark.

EMPIRE

The endangered bald eagle is soaring
Away from extinction, according to the evening news—
Good news after the news, after
The stocking masks and the blindfolds,
Contorted and disfigured nature in the dying days of oil.
What a surprise happy ending for the half hour.
Eagles airlift above the timberline—*cut to*
Their chicks nesting in the rocks.

The TV anchorman who predigests it all,
Himself has a great American carnivore prow,
But he is more an oak than an eagle.
According to polls, our father image comforts like the breast,
Is more trusted than the President by far.
Oh so honestly Carter's eyes widen and glitter
For emphasis—the expression of a very sober child
Who is showing you he can wiggle his ears.

Flags fly at half-mast all over the nation
For the fallen, each flagpole a pinprick,
So many pinpricks it becomes pain—
Three thousand continental miles from sea to sea
Reforested with half-flying flags. How unsuitable
For being on its knees Old Glory is,
Bomb burst and cheer on its knees under
Incomparable American skies, the famous North American light.

The famous humidity. Condensation frosts the bottom inch
Of the windshield, the first air conditioner day.
A rainbow of stainless steel, the Gateway Arch,
Takes off and lands, takes off and lands, takes off
And rises sixty stories, and swoops back and lands
A little way down the levee. A railroad bridge
Filigrees across the brown sumptuous river.
Humid flags sog at half-mast.

Bitter bitter bitter bitter
Cries a bird somewhere out over the river
At dusk, as darkness filters down through the soft evening
On Ste. Genevieve, near St. Louis. Remember,
The creek out there somewhere in the dark
Burbles, remember. You cannot see:
But close your eyes anyway, and smell.
The houses when you open your eyes are watching the news

Unshaved men in suits walk ahead of others in masks.
It might be the men one sees strolling
Together outside Claridge's in London followed
At a submissive distance by their veiled wives,
But in Central America—hostages and their slaves
By relay satellite. Rank as the odor in urine
Of asparagus from the night before,
This is empire waking drunk, and remembering in the dark.

THE NEW COSMOLOGY

Above the Third World, looking down on a fourth:
Life's aerial photograph of a new radio telescope
Discoloring an inch of mountainside in Chile,
A Martian invasion of dish receivers.
The tribes of Israel in their tents
Must have looked like this to God—
A naive stain of wildflowers on a hill,
A field of ear trumpets listening for Him,
Stuck listening to space like someone blind . . .

If there was a God.
There never is.
Almond-eyed shepherd warriors
Softly pluck their harps and stare off into space,
And close their eyes and dream.
In one tent, the Ark;
The chip of kryptonite.
They dream a recurring dream
About themselves as superpowers, and their origin.

Man is the only animal that dreams of outer space,
Epitome of life on earth,
The divine mammal which can dream
It is the chosen people of the universe
No more. But once you have got up high enough to look down,
Once you have got out far enough to look back,
The earth seems to magnify itself
In intensely sharp focus against the black,
Beautiful blind eye milky blue.

That we are alone, that we are not, are unimaginable.
We turn a page of *Life*,
Lying open in the grass,
To a pink earthworm slowly crossing the Milky Way
At nearly the speed of light—red-shifted protein!
The rest is unimaginable,
Like the silence before the universe.
The last nanosecond of silence twenty billion years ago
Before the big bang is endless.

A ROW OF FEDERAL HOUSES

A row of Federal houses with one missing,
The radicals' bomb factory, now blue sky,
An elegantly preserved "landmark block"
Address the last quake of the Sixties' underground leveled;
Leaving a prize street with an empty lot
Worth its weight in caviar, stripped naked
Between the wound-pale windowless raw side walls
Of the neighbors, left homeless in a flash
Whose value grows and grows. The years roll by,
Gray as big grains of butter-sweet beluga,
Real estate booms. The lot is still empty.
The purchaser still waits for permission to build.
No yellow ribbons yet for the hostages, tied
To the door knockers, sashed around the trees,
Which will become the symbol of support
For them, the Americans held in Iran. Surreal,
The Shah's dying of cancer in Cairo; his body
Escaped the revolution only to find
His insides turning into caviar,
The peacock and his court of torturers.
Marvelous, how time takes care of things;
Shad are running in the river with their
Delicious roe after years of none,
And seemingly hopeless pollution. There is hope.
The Landmarks Commission tells the community
The latest compromise design succeeds,
Protects the past, the unity of the block,
Your wishes went into it, etc.,
The way the mind negotiates a dream.

Gradually, Versailles bricks up the hole;
A million-dollar Bastille seals it off;
Till fountains rise from the swimming pool that fills
The garden space and the vast moment when
The daughter whose parents were gone for the summer heard
A thud while shopping, knew her friends were dead,
Smiled at the cashier, blankly turned
And walked away in the silence before the sirens.

THAT FALL

The body on the bed is made of china,
Shiny china vagina and pubic hair.
The glassy smoothness of a woman's body!
I stand outside the open door and stare.

I watch the shark glide by . . . it comes and goes—
Must constantly keep moving or it will drown.
The mouth slit in the formless fetal nose
Gives it that empty look—it looks unborn;

It comes into the room up to the bed
Just like a dog. The smell of burning leaves,
Rose bittersweetness rising from the red,
Is what I see. I must be twelve. That fall.

A DIMPLED CLOUD

Cold drool on his chin, warm drool in his lap, a sigh,
The bitterness of too many cigarettes
On his breath: portrait of the autist
Asleep in the arms of his armchair, age thirteen,
Dizzily starting to wake just as the sun
Is setting. The room is already dark while outside
Rosewater streams from a broken yolk of blood.

All he has to do to sleep is open
A book; but the wet dream is new, as if
The pressure of *De Bello Gallico*
And Willa Cather face down on his fly,
Spread wide, one clasping the other from behind,
Had added confusion to confusion, like looking
For your glasses with your glasses on.

A mystically clear, unknowing trance of being . . .
And then you feel them—like that, his first wet dream
Seated in a chair, though not his first.
Mr. Hobbs, the Latin master with
A Roman nose he's always blowing, who keeps
His gooey handkerchief tucked in his jacket sleeve,
Pulls his hanky out, and fades away.

French, English, math, history: masters one
By one arrive, start to do what they do
In life, some oddity, some thing they do,
Then vanish. The darkness of the room grows brighter
The darker it gets outside, because of the moonlight.
O adolescence! darkness of a hole
The silver moonlight fills to overflowing!

If only he could be von Schrader or
Deloges, a beautiful athlete or a complete
Shit. God, von Schrader lazily shagging flies,
The beautiful flat trajectory of his throw.
Instead of seeking power, being it!
Tomorrow Deloges will lead the school in prayer,
Not that the autist would want to take his place.

Naked boys are yelling and snapping wet towels
At each other in the locker room,
Like a big swordfighting scene from *The Three Musketeers*,
Parry and thrust, roars of laughter and rage,
Lush Turkish steam billowing from the showers.
The showers hiss, the air is silver fox.
Hot breath, flashes of swords, the ravishing fur!—

Swashbuckling boys brandishing their towels!
Depression, aggression, elation—and acne cream—
The eco-system of a boy his age.
He combs his wet hair straight, he hates his curls,
He checks his pimples. Only the biggest ones show,
Or rather the ointment on them caked like mud,
Supposedly skin-color, invisible; dabs

Of peanut butter that have dried to fossils,
That even a shower won't wash away, like flaws
Of character expressed by their concealment—
Secrets holding up signs—O adolescence!
O silence not really hidden by the words,
Which are not true, the words, the words, the words—
Unless you scrub, will not wash away.

But how sweetly they strive to outreach these shortcomings,
These boys who call each other by their last names,
Copying older boys and masters—it's why
He isn't wearing his glasses, though he can't see.
That fiend Deloges notices but says nothing.
Butting rams, each looks at the other sincerely,
And doesn't look away, blue eyes that lie.

He follows his astigmatism toward
The schoolbuses lined up to take everyone home,
But which are empty still, which have that smiling,
Sweet-natured blur of the retarded, oafs
In clothes too small, too wrong, too red and white,
And *painfully* eager to please a sadist so cruel
He wouldn't even hurt a masochist.

The sadistic eye of the autist shapes the world
Into a sort of, call it innocence,
Ready to be wronged, ready to
Be tortured into power and beauty, into
Words his phonographic memory
Will store on silence like particles of oil
On water—the rainbow of polarity

Which made this poem. I put my glasses on,
And shut my eyes. O adolescence, sing!
All the bus windows are open because it's warm.
I blindly face a breeze almost too sweet
To bear. I hear a hazy drone and float—
A dimpled cloud—above the poor white and poorer
Black neighborhoods which surround the small airfield.

THE BLUE-EYED DOE

I look at Broadway in the bitter cold,
The center strip benches empty like today,
And see St. Louis. I am often old
Enough to leave my childhood, but I stay.

A winter sky as total as repression
Above a street the color of the sky;
A sky the same gray as a deep depression;
A boulevard the color of a sigh:

Where Waterman and Union met was the
Apartment building I'm regressing to.
My key is in the door; I am the key;
I'm opening the door. I think it's true

Childhood is your mother even if
Your mother is in hospitals for years
And then lobotomized, like mine. A whiff
Of her perfume; behind her veil, her tears.

She wasn't crying anymore. Oh try.
No afterward she wasn't anymore.
But yes she will, she is. Oh try to cry.
I'm here—right now I'm walking through the door.

The pond was quite wide, but the happy dog
Swam back and forth called by the boy, then by
His sister on the other side, a log
Of love putt-putting back and forth from fry

To freeze, from freeze to fry, a normal pair
Of the extremes of normal, on and on.
The dog was getting tired; the children stare—
Their childhood's over. Everyone is gone,

Forest Park's deserted; still they call.
It's very cold. Soprano puffs of breath,
Small voices calling in the dusk is all
We ever are, pale speech balloons. One death,

Two ghosts . . . white children playing in a park
At dusk forever—but we must get home.
The mica sidewalk sparkles in the dark
And starts to freeze—or fry—and turns to foam.

At once the streetlights in the park go on.
Gas hisses from the trees—but it's the wind.
The real world vanishes behind the fawn
That leaps to safety while the doe is skinned.

The statue of Saint Louis on Art Hill,
In front of the museum, turns into
A blue-eyed doe. Next it will breathe. Soon will
Be sighing, dripping tears as thick as glue.

Stags do that when the hunt has cornered them.
The horn is blown. Bah-ooo. Her mind a doe
Which will be crying soon at bay. The stem
Between the autumn leaf and branch lets go.

My mother suddenly began to sob.
If only she could do that now. Oh try.
I feel the lock unlock. Now try the knob.
Sobbed uncontrollably. Oh try to cry.

How easily I can erase an error,
The typos my recalling this will cause,
But no correcting key erases terror.
One ambulance attendant flashed his claws,

The other plunged the needle in. They squeeze
The plunger down, the brainwash out. Bah-ooo.
Calm deepened in her slowly. There, they ease
Her to her feet. White Goddess, blond, eyes blue—

Even from two rooms away I see
The blue, if that is possible! Bright white
Of the attendants; and the mystery
And calm of the madonna; and my fright.

I flee, but to a mirror. In it, they
Are rooms behind me in our entrance hall
About to leave—the image that will stay
With me. My future was behind me. All

The future is a mirror in which they
Are still behind me in the entrance hall,
About to leave—and if I look away
She'll vanish. Once upon a time, a fall

So long ago that they were burning leaves,
Which wasn't yet against the law, I looked
Away. I watched the slowly flowing sleeves
Of smoke, the blood-raw leaf piles being cooked,

Sweet-smelling scenes of mellow preparation
Around a bloodstained altar, but instead
Of human sacrifice, a separation.
My blue-eyed doe! The severed blue-eyed head!

The windows were wide-open through which I
Could flee to nowhere—nowhere meaning how
The past is portable, and therefore why
The future of the past was always now

A treeless Art Hill gleaming in the snow,
The statue of Saint Louis at the top
On horseback, blessing everything below,
Tobogganing the bald pate into slop.

Warm sun, blue sky; blond hair, blue eyes; of course
They'll shave her head for the lobotomy,
They'll cut her brain, they'll kill her at the source.
When she's wheeled out, blue eyes are all I see.

The bandages—down to her eyes—give her
A turbaned Twenties look, but I'm confused.
There were no bandages. I saw a blur.
They didn't touch a hair—but I'm confused.

I breathe mist on the mirror . . . I am here—
Blond hair I pray will darken till it does,
Blue eyes that will need glasses in a year—
I'm here and disappear, the boy I was . . .

The son who lifts his sword above Art Hill;
Who holds it almost like a dagger but
In blessing, handle up, and not to kill;
Who holds it by the blade that cannot cut.

ON WINGS OF SONG

I could only dream, I could never draw,
In Art with the terrifying Mrs. Jaspar
Whom I would have done anything to please.
Aquiline and aloof in the land of the button nose, her smile
Made her seem a witch, my goddess,
Too cool, too cold. She was my muse
Because she hardly spoke a word.

We used to pronounce her name to rhyme with Casbah,
Mimicking her fahncy Locust Valley lockjaw.
Say Christ through your nose!
Part of her allure and majesty and
Wonderful strange music for St. Louis certainly,
Though not as musical as her silence was. Casbah,
White flannels on a summer evening, Jasbah,

Endless lawn down to the sea. The accent
Was preposterous, the voice beautiful
Green running down to the sea nine hundred miles inland,
Preposterous. The accent
Was preposterous, her beautiful voice a
Bassoon, slow velvet cadence of the sound,
Shy but deep. Shy but deep. Clangs / The bell. Eliot.

The lips are drawn back slightly;
As if it had been hinged that way, the jaw doesn't quite close—

Actually, the opposite of lockjaw since it
Moves, and it doesn't close.
The very back of the throat without the use of the lips
Produces the bloated drawl of the upper class.
You hear it in a certain set, you see it in a certain scene,

Which has equivalents abroad who sound incredibly the same,
And bong the same aristocrat gong in their own languages.
The stag hunting gang in France who hunt on horseback.
Most aquiline being the honorary hunt servants
In livery and wearing tricorns, always
Dukes and such and others who
The very back of the throat without using the lips much.

It is an accent you can *see*—
That you could hear through soundproof glass from what
        you saw.
It is a sound you see in the Sologne when
The huntsman blows his haunting horn.
The hounds open their mouths. Silence. The servants in their
White breeches and long blue coats dismount. The
Stag stands in the water dropping tears of terror and
        exhaustion.

They do that when the hunt has them at bay.
The king is in his counting house counting out his money.
His head will be hacked off and saved;
The carcass goes to the dogs—after the servants drink the blood

And defecate. There is another accent, that goes to Harvard,
That anyone who does can have. My babysitter
Harold Brodkey will. One day I, too, I will.

The servants dip their fingers in
The blood and paint themselves, and smear each other's blouses,
With all the time in the world apparently until it's time. It's time
To pass the chalice and drink. They defecate
In their breeches, but their coats are quite long,
The flecks on their boots are only mud,
Everything I've written here is lies.

The flecks could be flecks of blood,
But the coattails completely hide the other. There's a smell.
Though there's the smell rising in silence
From the page, but that's a lie. Brodkey knows. Lies that rise.
Now my unseen neighbor in New York four blocks away.
He is finishing the novel, he knows
Il miglior fabbro means a bigger liar. Lies that rise.

Ab lo dolchor qu'al cor mi vai
Pound catches the thermals in every language, and soars.
Eliot rises in the pew to kneel.
When he opens his mouth it is a choir.
Les souvenirs sont cors de chasse
Dont meurt le bruit parmi les vents.
The cockpit voice recorder in its crashproof case remembers
        and sings.

Flesh and juice of the refreshing and delicious.
Inside a crashproof housing. But I don't recognize the voice.
This is your Captain. In the unisex soprano of children his age.
We are trying to restart the engines
On wings of song. The pilot giggles posthumously—
"You may kiss my hond," he drawls, for the last time
Holding a hond out to be kissed from this page. (Sound of crash.)

MORPHINE

What hasn't happened isn't everything
Until in middle age it starts to be.
Night-blooming jasmine, dreams—and when they bring
You out on stage there's silence. Now I see,
You tell the darkness which is watching you.
Applause. Then instantly a hush, a cough.
It was another darkness once you knew
You had a blindfold on. You took it off,
But this is darker—down an unlit street,
An unmarked street, the three blocks to the shore.
They call it Banyan Street, night air so sweet.
Too much increasingly turns into more—
This is the martyr's grove on Banyan Street.
You breathe a perfumed darkness, numberless
Perfumes. The glistening as wet as meat
Deliciousness of sinking in. The S
OS of it. But it's too late. You reach
The can't stop trembling yes oh yes of it—
Already when you're two blocks from the beach
You start to drown. Love ruled your White House. Sit,
You named your dog. Come, Sit; *sit*, Sit; was love.
Your head explodes although you hear a shot.
Then archaeology . . . below above—
Beneath amnesia, Troy. But you forgot.

ELMS

It sang without a sound: music that
The naive elm trees loved. They were alive.
Oh silky music no elm tree could survive.
The head low slither of a stalking cat,
Black panther darkness pouring to the kill,
Entered every elm—they drank it in.
Drank silence. Then the silence drank. Wet chin,
Hot, whiskered darkness. Every elm was ill.
What else is there to give but joy? Disease.
And trauma. Lightning, or as slow as lava.
Darkness drinking from a pool in Java,
Black panther drinking from a dream. The trees
Around the edge are elms. Below, above,
Man-eater drinking its reflection: love.

THE FINAL HOUR

Another perfect hour of emptiness.
The final hour, calm as a candle flame.
The evening, enlarging as it neared, became
A sudden freshness, stillness, then the yes,
The fragrant falling yes of summer rain.
The huge grew larger as it neared, the smile,
The smell of rain, and waited for a while,
And went away. Time spilled. It left no stain.

JANE CANFIELD (1897–1984)

"The speed of light is not the limit. We
Are free. We glide. Our superluminous
Velocity will take us far. For us,
The superluminous is only the
Beginning of our birth. How born we are.
Compared to how we started. Vast, oh vast.
A lifetime as the measure couldn't last,
The nearest destinations were too far:
A billion years to reach the one inside
You if you could—who holds you, whom you hold.
You kick the covers off asleep, are cold,
And someone covers you, is all. And glide
Off into space. Is all. Space curved by speed—
We really leave the light behind. But hark.
The infinite beginning in the dark
To sigh the universe out of its seed.
The speck that weighs more than the world. Before
The universe—which has no meaning—was
Before the singularity which does.
Invisible nonzero, and we soar.
We sigh from the beginning, and we soar.
We leave the light behind and soar. And soar."

THE LITTLE WHITE DOG

The way the rain won't fall
Applies a velvet pressure, voice-off.
The held-back heaviness too sweet, the redolence,
Brings back the memory.

Life watches, watches,
From the control room, through the soundproof window,
With the sound turned off,
The orchestra warming up, playing scales.

It listens to the glistening.
The humidity reels, headier than methanol.
Treelined sidestreets, prick up your leaves.
The oboe is giving the la to the orchestra.

Someone shoots his cuffs to show his cufflinks,
Yellow gold to match his eyes, and pays the check.
Someone else is eight years old.
Her humility is volatile.

And when they kiss, he can't quite breathe.
The electric clouds perspire.
It's meteorology, it's her little dress, it's her violin,
It's unafraid. It's about to.

A sudden freshness stirs then stills the air, the century.
The new jet-black conductor raises her baton.
The melody of a little white dog,
Dead long ago, starts the soft spring rain.

AIDS DAYS

I

"Perfection Eludes Us"

The most beautiful power in the world has buttocks.
It is always a dream come true.
They are big. They are too big.
Kiss them and spank them till they are scalding.
Till she can't breathe saying oh.
Till your hand is in love.
Till your eyes are raw.
Stockings and garter belt without underpants are
The secret ceremony but who would imagine
She is wearing a business suit. She is in her office. She merely
    touches
The high-tech phone. Without a word,
She lies down across the hassock and eases her skirt up.
How big it is.
Her eyes are closed. . . . She has the votes.
They know she does. They're waiting for her now next door.
The number is ringing.
She squeezes them together. She squeezes them together.
She presses herself against the hassock.
She starts to spank herself.

II

The American Sonnet

She has the votes; they know she does;
They're waiting for her now next door.
Her eyes are closed.
We were discussing the arms race when the moderator died,
Presumably a performance piece, was
What it's called. He said it is.
It actually wasn't so political was only
Broadcast without a live audience.
The telephone is warbling.
The secretary has allowed the call through which means
    the President
Herself is on the line.
Her dreams are calling her. The press will be there.
Her skirt is all the way up.
I am the epopt. Thou art the secret ceremony.

III

Aleph, Beth, Gimel, Daleth . . .

A man sits memorizing a naked woman—
A slot cut in a wall
Which has a metal slide which opens
When he puts a quarter in
Lets him look for hours.
It seems like hours.
He keeps forgetting what he sees.
He pays and stares
Into the brightly lit beyond
Dancing on a stage just beyond the wall, bare feet
On a level with his chin.
He looks up at it,
Without the benefit of music
Just standing there.
And then the music starts again.
The wall in which the slot is cut is curved.
So when the slot is open, besides a dance he sees
Curving away from him to either side an ocean liner row
Of little windows.
Prisoners in solitary confinement
Might get their meals through one of these—
Presumably behind each one a booth like his.
The open slots are dark.
A slot of darkness in the wall
Is someone.

Someone hidden is hunching there.
From some slots money waves.
The woman ripples over and squats
In front of it, her knees spread wide.
She takes the bill—
Sometimes she presses herself against the slot.
A man stays in a booth.
The door stays locked. The slot stays open.
He can't remember what he memorized.
It seems like hours.
It is too late.

IV

L'Hallali

Serve me the ice cream bitterer than vinegar
Beneath a royal palm covered with needles.
Tell me a love story that ends with acyclovir
Five times a day for five days.

You never had it so good.
He made me my dog which He took.
Houseflies and herpes He brings.
Buttery ice cream smooth as Vaseline.

Florida. Dawn. Five hundred clouds.
Anal chocolate turning pink.
Oxygen-rich, from an opened artery
In the warm water

In the claw-footed tub. Dawn
Spreads from Gorbachev these arms talks AIDS days.
Will it spread?
Venus on the half-shell, moist and pink rose of salt—

Belons 000 when they're freshest are as sweet.
Chincoteagues from the bay are as plump.
Freshly squeezed is as sweet.
This is your life. You live in France,

Klaus Barbie, in 1983, and '84, and '85, and '86, and '87.
And every day is the bissextus.
And every dawn is Hiroshima.
Hallali!

GETHSEMANE

My life.
I live with it.
I look at it.
My spied on, with malice.

It's my wife. It's my husband.
It sleeps with me.
I wake with it.
It doesn't matter.

If I'm unfaithful—if I drank too much—
It's me. It's mine. It's all legal.
I smell the back of my hand,
And like the smell.

Twenty-five years ago when I was still alive.
I was twenty-five.
My penis pants. My penis
Rises, hearing its name, like a dog.

I ought to cut it off
And feed it to itself.
Like the young bride in the Babel story
Forced to eat her husband's penis

By the peasant who has cut it off.
A railroad telegrapher and a peasant
On the White Army side have found some Jews.
Russia 1918.

Interior railroad boxcar.
The boxcar door is slid open from the outside
Like a slowly lifted guillotine blade.
There they are.

I am fifty today. I hold the little cape and sword.
I dedicate this bull
That I'm about to kill
To the crowd.

To the crowd.
To the crowd.
To the crowd.
To the crowd. To the crowd. To the.

STANZAS

I don't want to remember the Holocaust.
I'm *thick* of remembering the Holocaust.
To the best of my ability, I wasn't there anyway.
And then I woke.

My hands were showing me how they wash themselves.
They're clean. The heart is too. The hands are too.
They flush in unison like a row of urinals
Every few hours automatically. Two minutes Cockfoster's.
My heart was pure. And stood on a subway platform in London
Staring at the sign. One minute Cockfoster's.

I wasn't there anyway.
I don't believe in anything.
I was somewhere else
Screaming beneath an avalanche.

Skiers wearing miners' headlamps were not
Skiing down the mountain in the dark,
It would be beautiful. Seeds of light floating slowly on the dark
Downward without a prayer
Of finding any elephants to save because
The International Red Cross and the Roman Catholic Church
        had not.

I cannot move.
I move my face from side to side
To make a space to breathe. I cannot breathe.
The screaming stops.

EARLY SUNDAY MORNING

IN THE CHER

The solemn radiance
On the radio is Poulenc.

The boy soprano seems to dream
He doesn't breathe.
And then the much shyer wings,
Of new materials, that add enormous range.
Oh, the power of the perfume!

The boys choir glides high above
The airborne orchestra.
Sweetness poured calmly and with innocent
Translucency blown
Into a glass.

While it's still warm it cools.

The glass is warped
On purpose, beautifully.
Poulenc, Auric, Milhaud, et cetera. Les Six.
A champagne flute contains the tears of Christ.

For this is France.

The radio predicts the weather for the region with such charm.
Charm followed by more rain will crucify the harvest.

And it is cold. So far,
The summer day is pure
Boy soprano blue without a cloud.

The naive fields of sunflowers don't know they suffer.
Suffer the little sunflowers to come unto me.
Their childish big faces gaze at everyone with love.

They sing so sweetly in the cold. They sing completely.

Shy wings repeat the
Seven last words of Christ,
I don't feel anything but it hurts.
I'm typing this with fingers of cold wax.
I can see my breath in the salon.

In August,
With green leaves warbling liquids of birdsong,
We have reached the Pole.

The Poulenc ripples chastely as an eel
Off the shores of silence, immaculately
To the place where they press olives.

Jesus prostrates himself on the ground.
Jesus jaywalks through the perfumed night air
Back and forth. How sweet it smells.
He is dovening and stops.
Abba, Father.
He looks for them and finds them
Fast asleep, Peter especially. Could
You not watch with me one hour? They couldn't
Even stay awake.
They sleep in the dark.

Who when I thought my son was dying slept.
My son was dying slept.

There she was.

Who when I thought my son was dying slept
And slept while I paced,
While they performed the emergency operation.
For hours. But then I too.
Could you not watch with me one hour?
Can't wake from my life either.
I too must wake.

The sun streams in and makes
Sunbeams of my solid house.
Blond air is my igloo.
The houseflies cryogenically unfreeze
And regain consciousness in order to be flies.
Before they fly, they jitter-walk around and pause
To rub their two front legs together.

Androgynous Akhenaten is singing his hymn to the Aten.
The awed wide-eyed words rise
On the wings of my houseflies,
Franciscan in their intimacy which shook the earth.

The radio is singing Christ is risen.
The sunflowers are singing to the sun.

These words I say to you are sunflowers singing to the sun.

There was a God
With human chromosomes, nearly human. . . . I fly
Across the inland flatness of the Cher
In my old car, in love. I give you God. I fly my car.
I'm bringing God back to God.

It doesn't matter what happens.

And when I said my car was me, instantly
My dingy bronze Simca's alternator was broken, yesterday.

We overheat up to the red.
We'll try to float to a garage.

I'm going nowhere fast. The
Same old 66.
Same difference.
Shades of the past. It doesn't matter what happens.

Just outside the door,
The dear cur snores on its tires. It sleeps in la France profonde.
The centerlines are silver, the roads are gold, en Berry today.
Shed a joyous tear for me
And my bronze-colored pal.

I made a clearing. I meditated. I made a temple.
To meet you in.

Carved the everywhere of Buddha out
Of polished quiet.

And Krishna's smile. And Krishna's
Heavenly hands pressed together in candent greeting.

Introibo ad altare Dei.
You've put my eyes out so I will see.

The heat-seeking missile desires the faraway sun.
Thy pheromones invite thy suitor.

The radio announcer on France Musique
Is speaking so melodiously his words perspire,
That professional sugar sound I abhor, but I can't hear.
I am listening to the rustle of your long black dress
On the telephone last night as you pulled it up
A thousand miles away.
Someone could have walked in.
The husky hush of your voice.
Raise your evening gown for me forever.

THE LAST POEM IN THE BOOK

I don't believe in anything, I do
Believe in you, vanished particles of vapor,
Field of force,
Undressed, undimmed Invisible,
Losing muons and gaining other ones,
Counterrotations with your
Robed arms raised out straight to each side
In a dervish dance of eyes closed ecstasy,
Tireless, inhuman,
Wireless technology
Of a ghost,
Of a spinning top on its point,
Of a tornado perspiring forward a few miles an hour
Uprooting everything and smelling sweetly like a lawn.
It's that time of year.
It's that time of year a thousand times a day. A thousand times
    a day,
A thousand times a day,
You are reborn flying to outski
The first avalanche each spring,
And buried alive.

I went to sleep last night so I could see you.
I went to see the world destroyed. It was a movie.
I went to sleep that night so I could see you.
And then a drink and then to sleep.
That's Vermont.
The universe hung like a flare for a while and went out,

Leaving nothing, long ago.
Each galaxy at war exhaled
A firefly glow, a tiny quiet, far away . . .
On and off . . . worlds off and on—and then
The universe itself brightened, stared and went out.
I cannot see.
I will not wake though it's a dream.
I move my head from side to side.
I cannot move.
The nights are cold, the sun is hot,
The air is alcohol at that altitude
Three thousand miles from here—is here
Today a thousand times.
You haven't changed.

There is a room in the Acropolis Museum.
The korai smile silence.
The way a virus sheds. The way
A weave of wind-shear
And the willingness to share is the perfect friend
Every child invents for his very own. I don't know.
The Parthenon suddenly made me cry.
I saw it and I sobbed,
And it doesn't share.
I was so out of it
You came too close. I got too near
The temple, flying low. I got too near
The power, past the ropes. I touched the restoration work.

It could mean a loss of consciousness
In the right-hand seat to be with God.
The Early Warning Ground Proximity Indicator is flashing.
Never mind. I knew it was.
The alarm ah-ooga ah-ooga and the computer-generated
Voice says
And says and says Pull Up Pull Up Pull Up Pull Up.

You say come closer.
You say come closer.
I cannot move.
You say I have to whisper this. Come closer.
I want to hear.
There also is the way a virus sheds.
I want to see. And the ground whispers
Closer. In the Littré the other day and you were there
In the Petit Robert. Grévisse—Larousse—
Ten million years from now, will there be anything?
The rain came down convulsively on the dry land,
As if it would have liked to come down even harder,
Big, kind, body temperature
Shudderings, and on the far bank of the newborn river,
The joyous drumming of the native drums,
Making a tremendous sound twelve feet beneath the snow
Without an avalanche beeper in those days. It's true—
I don't believe in anything I *do*
Believe in, but I do believe in you
Moving your face from side to side to make a space to breathe.

I think I am crying on all my legs
From a dark place to a dark place like a roach.
I am running on the ground with my wings folded—
But now I am extending them,
Running across my kitchen floor and
Running down the Rue Barbet-de-Jouy,
Trying historically before it's too late to get into the air.
I have on my ten Huntsman suits,
And many shining shoes made to my last.
I believe in one Lobb.
Faites sur mesure. Everything
Fits my body perfectly now that I'm about to disappear.
I don't believe in anything.
Lightning touches intimately the sable starless. Thunder.
You start to breathe too much.
It starts to rain, in your intoxication.
Communism and capitalism go up in flames
And come back down as rain—I'm coming now—
But Greece stays parched.
I'm coming now.

I'm being thrown violently at the sky,
The deck of the carrier shrinking to a dot,
Thirty-some years ago
Suddenly catching sight of Chartres Cathedral miles away;
Horizon to horizon, a molten ocean
The beautiful urine color of vermeil,
Color and undercolor as with a fur;

Soaring stock-still above the windblown waves of wheat,
Dialing on the seemingly inexhaustible power.
Break it.
I swim over to the sealed
Aquarium window of the TV screen to try.
President of the United States descending the stairs
Of his helicopter pixels snap a salute at the American flag
Pixels. I turn the sound off
And the Marine band explodes.
I'm coming now.
I can't breathe.
I'm coming now to the conclusion that
Without a God. I'm coming now to the conclusion.

A NOTE ON THE TYPE

This book was set in Monotype Dante, a typeface designed by Giovanni Mardersteig. Conceived as a private type for the Officina Bodoni at Verona, Italy, Dante was originally cut only for hand composition by Charles Malin, the famous Parisian punchcutter, between 1946 and 1952. Its first use was in an edition of Boccaccio's *Trattatello in laude di Dante* that appeared in 1954. The Monotype Corporation's version of Dante followed in 1957. Although modeled on the Aldine type used for Pietro Cardinal Bembo's *De Aetna* in 1495, Dante is an entirely modern interpretation of that venerable face.

Composed by Heritage Printers, Inc.,
Charlotte, North Carolina

Printed and bound by Halliday Lithographers,
West Hanover, Massachusetts

Designed by Peter A. Andersen